ISBN 12-531-08542-4

THE MONASTERY
OF ST. CATHERINE
ON MOUNT SINAI

John F. Harriman, Ph.D.
1312 Fillmore Ave
Bellingham, WA 98225-6328

PUBLISHED by St. CATHERINE'S MONASTERY AT SINAI

TEXT by Athanasios Paliouras, Professor in the University of Ioannina
CAPTIONS by His Eminence Damianos Archbishop of Sinai
EDITORIAL SUPERVISION: Solon Tzaferis
DESIGN: Chryse Daskalopoulou
PHOTOGRAPHY: Nicolas Tzaferis
            Fathers of St. Catherine's Monastery at Sinai
TYPESETTING: Dimis Karras
COLOUR SEPARATION: Irida
MONTAGE: Alekos Ventouris
            PUBLISHED by St. CATHERINE'S MONASTERY AT SINAI - E. TZAFERI A.E.
                        Copyright © 1985
                              by
                    HIERA MONI SINA - E. TZAFERI
PRINTED IN GREECE by E. TZAFERI A.E.,
                    Leoforos Lavriou 78, GR-153 44
                    Glyka Nera Attikis, Greece
                    Tel. 6659632 - Telex 222453 TZAF GR
First Printing 1985: 10,000 copies
                    in Greek - Arabic - English - French - German - Italian
English Translation: Helen Zigada

Cover Plates: Front: View of St. Catherine's Monastery at Sinai.
            Back: Embroidered cross (pl. 79).

                                                    ISBN 960-429-001-0

FOREWORD

It is with great pleasure that the Holy Monastery of St. Catherine on Mount Sinai presents to the pious visitor a fairly descriptive and informative guide to this place of pilgrimage.

In this luxurious edition the illustrations of the holy sites, of the ancient buildings and, especially, of the numerous splendid icons, manuscripts and other relics tell even more than the accompanying text.

The overcoming of not a few technical and other problems has required hard work from many people and, of course, from the Fathers of the Monastery.

Warm thanks are due to all; in particular, to Mr. Solon Tzaferis and Mr. Nicholas Tzaferis, who have spared neither effort nor expense, travelling many times from Greece to Sinai in order to achieve the best possible result for this work which they edited and published. Warm thanks are also due to the Byzantinist Mr. Athanasios Paliouras, Professor in the University of Ioannina, Greece, who has kindly offered to write the text for this publication.

If, in addition to whatever artistic enjoyment this volume may offer, the tired wayfarer of today's hectic life derives some spiritual pleasure and a sense of peace in God, the main purpose of this work will have been attained and our gratitude to our Patroness Saint Catherine and our Lord Jesus Christ will be even greater and everlasting.

With blessings,
Damianos, Archbishop of Sinai

THE MONASTERY OF ST. CATHERINE ON MOUNT SINAI

A BRIEF HISTORICAL OUTLINE

The Sinai Desert

The triangular area between the Desert of El-Tih, the Gulf of Suez and the Gulf of Aqabah is a wilderness of granite rock and rugged mountains, forbidding and inaccessible at first sight. For centuries now, this desert land has been scorched by the blazing sun during days and frozen by the cold of silent nights.

Small towns and villages have grown on the shores of the two gulfs, but only a few Bedouin nomads roam the mountainous and arid inland of the Sinai Peninsula. The desert has very few small valleys, like the Oasis of Faran, with scant water and little cultivable land yielding a limited produce of vegetables and dates, which provide sustenance to the wandering Bedouin families and their flocks.

Famous massive mountains dominate the peninsula: Mount Sinai (2,285 m.), Mount Um Shamer, Mount of St. Catherine (2,637 m.), Mount Serbal (2,070 m.), Mount of St. Episteme.

The Journey of the Israelites

It is through this wilderness that Moses led the Israelites from the Red Sea to Palestine, the Promised Land. Moses had to provide water and food for his people and to repulse the constant attacks of the Amalekites, the nomadic tribe of Arabia who fought the Israelites. The inspired personality of Moses and God's miraculous providence (with an inexhaustible supply of quail and «manna») sustained the people of Israel for forty years in this barren and wild desert land.

It is in this wilderness, on the summit of Mount Sinai which nearly touches the fringes of Heaven, that God and man met again. «*And the Lord came down upon Mount Sinai, on the top of the mount: and the Lord called Moses...*» (Ex. 19,20). «*And he gave unto Moses... tables of stone, written with the finger of God.*» (Ex. 31, 18).

Before this great moment for mankind and the history of the world, Moses had met with the angel of God: «*And the angel of the Lord appeared unto him in a flame of fire out of the midst of a bush: And he looked and, behold, the bush burned with fire, and the bush was not consumed... And God called unto him out of the midst of the bush and said, Moses, Moses... put off thy shoes from off thy feet, for the place whereon thou standest is holy ground... And he said, I am the God of thy father, the God of Abraham, the God of Isaac and the God of Jacob.*» (Ex. 3, 2-6).

Thus, the arid and desolate Sinai desert became a holy place sacred to mankind. The historian K. Amantos notes that «in all the ancient world there exists no place so poor and insignificant that has become so holy and legendary as Sinai in Arabia».

Monastic life

Monastic life started very early in this region. Christian hermits began to gather at Sinai from the middle of the 3rd century. St. Antony's retreat into the desert in the early 4th century prompted many hermits to settle at the foot of Mount Sinai and also of the other mountains, in particular Mount Serbal, where they led a life of strict spiritual and corporal discipline.

The solitary life and spiritual practice of the hermits went through great hardships in the 4th and 5th centuries. These were increased further by the persecutions they suffered from barbarian assailants «who sacrificed camels to their gods and did not refrain from slaughtering Christian monks».

The monk Ammonius of Egypt wrote *A discourse upon the Holy Fathers slain on Mount Sinai and at Raitho.* This was translated into the so-called «simple Greek» tongue (a mixture of vernacular and ancient Greek used in scholarly texts) by the monk Agapios Landos of Crete, who included it in the *New Paradise.* Another celebrated ascete and author of the 5th century, St. Nilus of Sinai, wrote *Tales on the slaying of the monks on Mount Sinai and on the captivity of his son Theodoulos.* This work was translated recently into «simple Greek» under the title *Lament for Theodoulos* by the theologian Athanasios Kottadakis.

However, the massacre and martyrdom of the Holy Fathers of Sinai and Raitho by the Hagarenes and the Blemmyes of Africa in Diocletian's reign did not affect the development of monasticism in the Sinai desert. The anchorite population of South Sinai grew and the fame of many of the hermits spread to both East and West.

Small monastic communities were formed quite early, especially in the area of Mount Horeb, the site of the Burning Bush and the valley of Faran (ancient Pharan). The anchorites lived in caves, stone-built cells and huts, spending their days in silence, prayer and sanctity.

It is reported that in A.D. 330, in response to a request by the ascetics of Sinai, the Byzantine empress Helena (St. Helen) ordered the building of a small church consecrated to the Holy Virgin at the site of the Burning Bush and of a fortified enclosure where the hermits could find refuge from the incessant attacks of primitive pagan nomadic tribes.

From the 4th century onwards South Sinai became a place of pilgrimage visited by many pilgrims from far-away lands. A manuscript discovered in 1884 relates that in A.D. 372-374 Aetheria, a noblewoman from Spain accompanied by a retinue of clerics, journeyed to Sinai to visit the hermits. Aetheria found a small church on the summit of Mount Sinai, another one on Mount Horeb and a third one at the site of the Burning Bush, near which there was a fine garden with plenty of water.

Aetheria's account revealed the expansion of monasticism in the Sinai desert. By the middle of the 5th century the growing population of hermits was apparently headed by a dignitary, mentioned as Bishop of Pharan. With the passing of time this office and title were taken over by the Bishop of Sinai. On more than one occasion the monks of Sinai struggled for the consolidation of the Orthodox faith by taking an active part in the controversies between Church and heretics.

When monasticism in the Sinai peninsula expanded, men of great moral stature emerged from this arid and desolate place. Apparently in response to a request by the Sinaites, Justinian, emperor of Byzantium, founded a magnificent church, which he enclosed within walls strong enough to withstand attacks and protect the monks against eventual raids.

The historian Procopius in his work *On Buildings* has preserved useful information on the church and the «very strong fortress» built by Justinian.

Henceforth, a new glorious page begins in the holy history of Sinai.

The fortress of Justinian

The fortified enclosure of the Monastery is built of rectangular hewn blocks of hard granite. It is somewhat off-square in shape, its sides measuring 75 m. on the west, 88 m. on the north, 75 m. on the east and 80 m. on the south. The height varies from 8 m. on the south to 25 m. on the north side, and the thickness of the granite wall ranges from 2 to 3 m., depending on the space needed for towers, crypts etc. The south wall, decorated on the outer side with ancient cross symbols and other stone carvings, faces towards Mount Sinai and is the one that has been best preserved. The north wall has suffered the worst damages and has been repaired several times over the centuries, even by Napoleon's army in 1798-1801.

The ancient gate, with a machicolation above it to strengthen its defence, is on the west side of the fortress. Today this gateway is closed, and another old entrance is in use, secured every night by three iron-bound doors.

The monks' cells and other structures were built along the inner sides of the fortified enclosure. The irregular and sloping ground was levelled by constructing solid arches and barrel-vaults, upon which the monks' dwellings and other buildings were raised.

The Monastery's Church (Katholikon), also built at that time of massive granite blocks, is a three-aisled basilica with narthex. It measures 40 m. in length and 19.20 m. in width, including the chapels it incorporates behind the sanctuary apse, i.e. the Chapel of the Burning Bush and the terminal chapels dedicated to St. James and to the Holy Fathers of Sinai. The naos proper of the Katholikon measures 25 m. in

length and 12 m. in width. It is divided into three aisles by colonnades of six monolithic granite columns, each carrying a different capital ornamented with cross, lamb, plant and fruit motifs. The columns have been covered with a coating so that the beautiful colour of the granite stone is no longer visible.

In the 18th century, during the time when Cyril of Crete was Archbishop of Sinai, the ancient timber roof of the Katholikon was covered with a horizontal wooden coffered ceiling, which was painted blue and adorned with a multitude of golden stars. The side walls are pierced by two rows of windows – eight double – arched windows and seven rectangular ones. The level of the holy bema is higher than that of the nave. The templon separating these two areas of the church is composed of marble panels below and a woodcarved iconostasis above, reaching to the ceiling with the so-called *Lypera* (icons of the Virgin and St. John standing on either side of the Crucifix). The iconostasis is of the early 17th century, made in 1612 in the Monastery's dependency of Crete at the time of the Archbishop Lavrentios.

The original splendidly carved doors leading from the narthex to the naos proper are made of Lebanon cedar wood and date from the 6th century. The portal of the narthex was made by the Crusaders in the 11th century.

The church is decorated with rare and priceless icons of various periods.

Inscriptions

The surviving inscriptions recording the names of Justinian and Theodora indicate that the fortress and the church were built in A.D. 557, after the death of the empress. This date is indirectly confirmed by the writings of Cosmas Indicopleustes, who lived in the Sinai peninsula before A.D. 548, and mentions the monastery at Pharan but not that at Mount Sinai. Inscriptions, both early and later, are found on the roof beams, on the carved doors of the naos and on the lintel of the outer portal of the church. From the inscriptions we learn that Stephanos of Aila (the present-day Elath) was architect of the fortress and church of the Monastery.

Sinai and Mohammed the founder of Islam

In the 7th century the Monastery of Sinai faced a dangerous situation and a grave crisis, mainly due to the Arab conquest. Although information on those times is scant, we are told by a source referring to the year 808 that the number of the Monastery's monks had been reduced to thirty, while religious life on the Sinai peninsula, where thousands of anchorites had once dwelt, was all but extinct. At all events, Justinian's fortress and church, the sacred relics, the precious icons and

manuscripts survived these troubled times. Something must have occurred to allow the Monastery of Sinai to go through the general upheaval that swept the regions of Egypt and Syria and continue on its holy course.

According to tradition and as deduced from indirect information, the Fathers of the Monastery requested the protection of Mohammed for the Sinaites and for the Christians and Jews living at Raitho and Aila. The request was favourably accepted and by the so-called *ahtiname* or «immunity covenant» Mohammed instructed his followers to protect the monks of Sinai, thus saving them from eventual danger and destruction. This document has been a matter of controversy among 20th century scholars, for some supported its authenticity while others – particularly a number of Arabists – assigned it to a date after A.D. 900. However, as the historian K. Amantos rightly suggests, «the Monastery of Sinai could not possibly have survived without the protection afforded by Mohammed and his successors... Moreover, the great number of decrees which the Mohammedan rulers of Egypt issued confirming the protected status of the Monastery must have resulted from the fact that Mohammed himself had granted protection to Sinai.»

It is reported that when Sultan Selim I conquered Egypt and Sinai in 1517, he was shown Mohammed's «immunity covenant», which he took along leaving a copy to the Fathers of Sinai. Copies of the document have been preserved to this day in the Monastery.

The monks of Sinai, therefore, continued their historical course, observing the rules of asceticism and following the precepts of spiritual life. Parallel to their religious practice, they exercised the traditional byzantine philanthropy, helping with food, clothing and money the Bedouins who served the Monastery on a permanent basis, often carrying provisions by camels from Raitho (present-day El-Tor), Gaza or Suez.

Sinai and the West

The 11th century marks a new period for the monks of Sinai. The transfer of relics of St. Catherine to France and the presence of Crusaders at Sinai (1099-1270) spurred the interest of European Christians for the security and independence of the monks and for the safeguard of the land properties (dependencies) owned by the Monastery in Egypt, Palestine, Syria, Crete, Cyprus and Constantinople.

During the Frankish rule of Syria, the Crusaders founded a special order, the «Knights of Sinai», for the protection and financial assistance of the Monastery of Sinai. The carved wooden portal giving access to the narthex of the Katholikon and the various latin inscriptions in the old Refectory are dating from those years. During the same period the Monastery had a Moslem garrison, and the Sinai Fathers had to maintain a delicate balance between the Christians of the West and the Moslem Arabs of the region.

The Popes of Rome have at times defended the rights of the Monastery with various bulls and proclamations. Pope Honorius III in 1217, Pope Gregory X (1271-1276), Pope John XXII (1316-1334), Pope Benedict XII in 1358, Pope Innocent VI in 1360, have in many ways expressed their good-will and interceded in favour of the Monastery's privileges in Crete, Cyprus and other places.

Similarly, the Doges of Venice regulated with official documents the attitude of the Dukes of Crete concerning the Monastery's dependencies on the island. They also ruled in favour of the monks' interests, granted tax exemptions, and occasionally permitted even the collection of funds in aid of the Monastery.

The Venetians, as well as other Christians of the West, respected the Monastery's ships, which sailed the seas flying the banner of St. Catherine with the Saint's monogram (AK).

Relations between Sinai and Byzantium: Sinai «our pride»

Although Sinai was situated in a Mohammedan region, communication with Constantinople never stopped and relations with Byzantium were close. There are records of decisions and actions by a number of Byzantine emperors extending financial assistance and enjoining respect for the Monastery of Sinai, «the ark of Orthodox tradition». The emperors Manuel Comnenos and Michael Palaeologos, as well as Patriarchs of the See of Constantinople, manifested great interest in the affairs and problems of this very ancient Christian monastery. The capital's frequent communication with such eminent Sinaites as St. George Arselaus, St. John Climacus and St. Gregory of Sinai discloses the spiritual links between these two centres of Orthodoxy. Besides, the association of the well-known ateliers and scriptoria of Constantinople with those of Sinai, and the regular correspondence between Fathers of the Monastery and persons of rank in the Byzantine capital bear witness to the close collaboration between Sinai and Byzantium.

The official attitude and opinion of the Byzantines regarding the Monastery and its prestige is epigrammatically expressed in a letter by the Patriarch of Constantinople Gennadios (1454), addressed to «the most honourable among monks Kyr Maximos, by his worldly name Sophianos, and to all the most blessed hieromonks and monks practising asceticism in the holy Monastery of Sinai». The Patriarch calls Sinai «our pride», thereby indicating the great esteem and reverence in which the Orthodox held the oldest Christian monastery in the world.

Sinai and the Ottoman Turks

Turkish Sultans, in particular Selim I and Suleiman the Magnificent, had at times issued favourable decrees exempting the Monastery from custom duties and helping it attain great prosperity. On several occasions Turkish Sultans defended the interests of the Monastery against the claims of powerful Jews on Sinai. During the same period the Christian kings of Europe and other important rulers gave financial assistance and presented the Monastery with generous donations.

In the 16th and 17th centuries, on the Venetian-ruled island of Crete, the School of Letters of the Monastery's Dependency of St. Catherine at Herakleion acquired great fame and was attended by some notable men of that age.

Sinai and Napoleon

When Napoleon conquered Egypt in 1798, he placed the Monastery at Sinai under his protection, at the request of the Sinaites. The document confirming the protected status – now kept in the Monastery's Gallery – recognized older privileges and consolidated the autonomy of the Monastery and the region. Napoleon also recognized the Monastery's properties in Cairo and granted the Sinaites certain rights that permitted them to oppose arbitrary acts and defend against plunder in a more effective way.

THE ICONS: ART TREASURES OF FIFTEEN CENTURIES

The Monastery of St. Catherine at Sinai has one of the most important icon collections in the world. Over 2,000 icons, large and small, unique masterpieces and simple works of art, are kept in the Katholikon, the chapels, the icon gallery, the sacristy, the monks' cells and other parts of the Monastery. These icons cover a very long span of time from the 6th to the 19th century. Every period (Early Christian, Byzantine, post-Byzantine) has added new treasures enriching the Monastery's vast collection.

Encaustic icons

The so-called encaustic icons are of great historical and artistic value. The encaustic technique employs wax and vegetal pigments mixed at a high temperature and spread on a wooden surface. The artist made a preliminary drawing of the subject on the wooden (or very rarely marble) panel, and applied the still warm mixture to the surface by means of a brush or a hot iron. He then worked on the colours rubbing the mixture into the painted surface with the help of a special instrument. The mixture penetrated deeply into the pores of the material and when it cooled the colours became indelible.

The encaustic technique had been known from early antiquity and had been used until the 7th century A.D., when it was replaced by the so-called secco (or

tempera) painting. The famous portraits of the dead found in great numbers at Faiyum in Middle Egypt (2nd-4th century A.D.) were executed in the encaustic technique. The Monastery of Sinai has a number of encaustic icons, of which the most important are the following eight:

1. *St. Peter* (0.52 × 0.39 m.). The Saint is portrayed with large wide-open eyes, short grey hair and short well-groomed beard, holding a cross in the left hand and three keys in the right. The face is painted in the tradition of the encaustic Faiyum portraits of Alexandrian art. The Saint's head is surrounded by a large golden halo. The top of the icon is occupied by three small medallions. The middle one, with a cross in the background, contains a portrait of Christ and the right one a portrait of the Virgin. The identification of the beardless youth portrayed in the third medallion has posed a problem to scholars. Sotiriou presented two versions, proposing an identification with either Moses or St. John the Evangelist. Weitzmann maintains that the figure should be identified as St. John the Evangelist, because it appears to correspond to that of the Virgin on the right of the crucified Christ. Besides, the depiction of these particular holy figures in the three medallions may be interpreted as a representation of the Crucifixion, and linked with the obvious symbolism of the cross in St. Peter's hand, which can but allude to the Saint's death on the cross.

Sotiriou relates this icon of St. Peter with the three medallions to consular diptychs (emperor - empress - consuls= Christ - the Virgin - Peter and John) and dates the icon to the 6th century, without excluding a possible dating in the 5th century. Weitzmann believes that this splendid icon of St. Peter, with the sad but grave and composed expression, was painted in a Constantinopolitan atelier in the late 6th or early 7th century.

2. *The Virgin and Child enthroned between Saints and Angels* (0.70 × 0.49 m.). This outstanding icon has survived in two pieces, unskilfully joined together with wire. It represents the Virgin enthroned, supporting the Child Christ in her lap and flanked by two warrior Saints, the bearded St. Theodore Stratelates on the right and the beardless St. George on the left, both standing in formal pose. Two Archangels are pictured behind the central group, their wide-open eyes staring with awe at the hand of God which descends from heaven emitting a beam of light towards the head of the Holy Virgin. Portrayed frontally, on a slightly larger scale than the rest of the figures composing the icon, the Virgin is seated on the red cushion of the pearl-studded throne, dressed in a dark blue *maphorion* (veil), her feet in purple shoes resting on a golden footrest adorned with pearls. An intense realism is reflected in the Virgin's white and pink face painted with ample highlights and green shades, in her strongly accentuated features and large dissimilar eyes with their vivid glance. The Christ Child is pictured seated in a remarkably easy and comfortable pose on His mother's lap. The two Archangels, with their different haloes but otherwise perfectly uniform treatment and classical rendering, form a splendid complement to the central group.

Generally speaking, this icon presents a synthesis of the hieratic character of religious art and the profound meaning of theological doctrine. It symbolizes the mystery of the incarnation of Christ made man and the glory of the Mother of God. This justifies the intense expression of the countenances, the solemn attitudes of the Saints present at the glory of the Mother of God, the awed attention of the Archangels who «behold» the mystery of the incarnation.

The icon is dominated by the formal severity and hieratic character of monumental art in Justinian's age. It also reflects the splendour of the imperial court, particularly in the Saints' attires, and clearly betrays the continuation of Hellenistic tradition in the treatment of the Archangels. This masterpiece, therefore, has been dated by most scholars (Weitzmann, Kitzinger) in the age of Justinian and attributed to an imperial atelier of Constantinople. On the other hand, G. and M. Sotiriou maintain that this icon is a Syro-Palestinian work.

3. *Christ Pantocrator* (0.85 × 0.45 m.). This is an early type of the Christ Pantocrator. Wearing a tunic (*chiton*) and a draped outer garment (*himation*), Christ makes the sign of blessing with the right hand and holds in the left a very thick Gospel-book with a cover adorned with jewels and precious stones. The eyes are not alike in size and shape, the mouth is asymmetrical with a melancholy expression, the rather short beard has an inward curve and the hair falls back over the left shoulder.

The exceptionally high quality of the painted icon suggests that it must have been the product of a Constantinopolitan atelier in Justinian's age. This may be further confirmed by the fact that the iconographical type it represents was created at the time when Justinian was emperor, although we cannot be absolutely certain about that. It should be remembered at this point that the Monastery at Sinai had been founded by Justinian and that the emperor had presumably sent various gifts to the Monastery, including perhaps this fine icon of Christ Pantocrator.

G. and. M. Sotiriou had dated the icon to the 13th century. However, its cleaning and conservation in 1962 revealed the original encaustic layer, thus pointing to a much earlier date in the 6th (or more likely the 7th) century.

4. *The Virgin Paraklesis* (0.65 × 0.40 m.). The icon has suffered severe damage and is now composed of four surviving pieces of the broken wooden panel. The part where the eyes had been painted is now destroyed and along with it the main feature that would have given an indication of the Virgin's expression. In the right hand the Virgin holds an unrolled scroll containing her conversation with Christ in verse. Portrayed with the head inclined and the left hand placed before the breast, the Virgin is of the type known in Byzantine art as «Hagiosoritissa» – though when carrying an inscription of prayer, as in this case, the type would be more appropriately accompanied by the epithet «Paraklesis». In all probability this icon of the Virgin was one of the two wings of a diptych, the other being an icon of Christ to whom she addresses her prayer.

The icon is dated in the pre-iconoclastic period, notably the late 6th or early 7th century, and is a product of a Constantinopolitan atelier. It was repeatedly painted over in the 13th century.

5. *Christ Pantocrator* (0.35 × 0.21 m.). Wooden encaustic icon kept in the Monastery's old Library. The unpainted border and the nail-holes betray the existence of a frame that had once protected the icon. The bad state of preservation makes difficult the study of details. The portrayal of Christ is frontal and in bust form. The face is triangular in shape, the right hand emerges from the opening of the outer garment making the sign of blessing, the left hand, no longer visible, holds a Gospel-book with gold ornaments on the cover. It is difficult to trace the provenance of the icon. Some scholars (Sotiriou) are in favor of a «Syro-Palestinian» origin, others (Weitzmann, Grabar) maintain that the icon could be attributed to a Constantinopolitan atelier.

6. *The Ascension* (0.46 × 0.30 m.). The icon is broken in two pieces. The vertical break has destroyed the central points of the original representation. The figures of Christ in the oval mandorla, above, and of the Virgin standing among the Apostles, below, were repainted in an artless manner at a much later time. The remaining figures from the original phase of painting (the four angels carrying the «glory» of Christ, the left half of the group of Apostles and the last Apostle of the other half), as well as parallels from illuminated manuscripts and from Ascension scenes on some Monza ampullae (i.e. little flasks containing blessed oil presented to pilgrims to the Holy Places) point to a Syro-Palestinian workshop of the 6th century.

7. *Christ Emmanuel* (0.76 × 0.53 m.). Christ is portrayed in a «glory», seated on the arc of heaven and resting His feet on an arc of white rays. Dressed in *chiton* and *himation*, He makes the sign of blessing with the right hand and holds an open Gospel-book in the left hand. Four cherubim encircle the «glory» surrounding the figure of Christ. His white hair and beard are in contrast to the inscription EMMA-NOYHΛ, which accompanies as a rule the type of the young beardless Christ. But the apocalyptic Christ in «glory», carried by four cherubim or by the symbols of the four Evangelists, is associated with Isaiah's and Ezekiel's vision of the Ancient of Days whose hair was «as white as wool».

In brief, we can say that this icon combines the three «manifestations» of Christ:
a) as «the Ancient of Days» (Christ in eternity, denoted by the white hair and beard)
b) as «Christ Pantocrator» (blessing and holding the Gospel-book)
c) as «Emmanuel» (the incarnate Logos of God, denoted by the inscription O EMMANOYHΛ).

As far as its origin is concerned, Weitzmann and Chatzidakis maintain that the icon is an Egyptian work, whereas the Sotiriou believe that it is the product of a Constantinopolitan atelier because it reflects an obvious influence from the Classical Greek tradition.

8. *The Three Youths in the Fiery Furnace* (0.35 × 0.50 m.). The three youths, Hananiah, Azariah and Mishael, are dressed in Persian costumes. They are depicted standing in a row amid the red flames of the furnace, their heads surrounded by large haloes with red circles. At the left end an angel with a long cross-bearing

sceptre touches with the left hand Hananiah's shoulder. The colour scheme of the painting, the frontal pose, absence of massiveness and simplified almost linear contours of the figures, which minimize any form of depth, reduce the impression of material reality and enhance the hieratic character of the composition. The icon is stylistically related to the encaustic marble panels painted with the representations of Abraham and Jephthah in the sanctuary of the Monastery's Katholikon. This points to a dating in the 7th century and confirms the Palestinian origin of the icon.

From Sinai to Russia

In the middle of the 19th century, Porphyrius Ouspensky, Bishop of Kiev, artfully got hold of the following four encaustic icons from the Sinai collection. These were subsequently transported to Russia and are now exhibited in the Kiev Museum.

1. St. John the Baptist (0.47 × 0.25 m.). The Forerunner is portrayed full length, turning towards the miniature image of Christ depicted in the upper left-hand corner. The upper right-hand corner contains a miniature representation of the Virgin, also turning towards Christ. This icon is therefore an early form of the Deesis, dated to the 5th or 6th century.

2. The Virgin and Child (0.35 × 0.20 m.). The icon, which is distinguished for the inwardness and high spirituality reflected in the portraits of the Theotokos and of the Christ Child, is a Constantinopolitan work dated to the 6th century.

3. Sts. Sergius and Bacchus (0.28 × 0.49 m.). The two martyrs, who had been officers of the imperial court, are depicted frontally, with a small medallion containing the bust of Christ at the centre. The icon seems to be rather of Constantinopolitan origin, possibly dating from the early 7th century.

4. St. Platon and an unknown female martyr (0.45 × 0.49 m.). The two martyrs are shown in bust, holding a cross in their hand, their faces reflecting a profound spirituality. The painting is considered as one of the earliest examples of group portraiture in the history of portable icons. It is attributed to a Syro-Palestinian workshop and is dated to the 6th or 7th century.

Icons of monastic Eastern art of the 7th-9th century

The icons of this group have come from local workshops active in monasteries of the East, particularly Egypt, Palestine, Syria and Cappadocia. They are dated in the period from the 7th to the 9th century, when the Arab conquest precluded all contact of the Eastern regions with the Greek centres. These paintings are products of a folk art of less refined character, which makes use of a primitive realism to give expression to the local tradition of the Coptic and Syrian Churches. It should be remembered, however, that these rare icons dating from the first millennium have been one of the main sources that contributed in shaping Christian art in the following centuries.

An outstanding icon of this group depicting the Crucifixion shows Christ with His eyes closed, clad in a long purple colobium.

Icons dating from the 9th to the 12th century

The icons of this period present two characteristic developments. First, they illustrate the continuation of pre-iconoclastic painting tradition into the post-iconoclastic period, and second, they show a turn towards the classical concept of art, reflected in the delicacy of drawing and the beauty of form.

These important icons, many of which have come from the imperial ateliers of Byzantium, include one with scenes from the story of King Abgar, where we find the earliest representation of the Holy Mandylion, and others with portrayals of Christ, depictions of Archangels, Saints, hierarchs and hermits, scenes from the Twelve Feasts cycle (*Dodecaorton*) and from the lives of Saints.

Illuminated manuscripts, including Gospel-books, synaxaries and other texts, were produced in great numbers during this period, and the very significant art of miniature painting had a more general influence on iconography.

Icons of the Comnenian age (1080-1200)

In the Comnenian age icon-painting was continued in the great tradition of the earlier Macedonian school, with works of classicist tendency, provincial character or monastic inspiration, depending on the place and environment from which they originated. The Monastery of Sinai possesses a large collection of icons from this period, representative of all three trends. The beholder is impressed by the well-balanced layout of compositions, the forceful expression of figures, the harmony of colour schemes, the tendency towards dematerialization combined with a refined sense of nobility and grace.

Outstanding examples are «the Virgin enthroned surrounded by Prophets», «the Great Deesis and scenes from the Dodecaorton», «the Crucifixion in a frame containing busts of Saints», the excellent representation of «the Miracle at Chonae», a most expressive icon of «Christ Pantocrator», splendid mosaic icons like that of «the Virgin Hodegetria», powerful depictions of the Archangels Michael and Gabriel, fine portrayals of Saints (especially that of St. Nicholas), and scenes from the life, miracles and Passion of Christ.

Icons on iconostasis epistyles

These icons were painted as a frieze along the entire length of the upper part or epistyle of wood-carved icon-screens. Most of them have come from the various chapels of the Monastery and are dated from the 11th to the 14th century. The most important example (which has a total length of 2.75 m.) is composed of eleven scenes from the life of St. Eustratios.

The subjects usually depicted in epistyle icons are the Great Deesis, scenes from the Dodecaorton (cycle of the Twelve Feasts), scenes from the life of the Virgin and miracles of Saints. The paintings are executed in a masterly technique and admirable colour scale, the figures are portrayed with spiritual intensity and lively movement. Generally speaking, the icons of this group reveal a workmanship of high artistic standard with marked traces of a great tradition in icon-painting.

Menologia

The so-called *menologia*, i.e. depictions of the Saints honoured on each day of the ecclesiastical year, form another large and significant category of icons in the Monastery of Sinai. These are of various types: twelve large icons, composed of full-length portraits of the Saints of each month; two large icons, in diptych form, comprising all the Saints of the ecclesiastical year; a four-wing icon and a twelve-wing icon of Saints and Martyrs, portrayed in successive rows, the former standing and the latter suffering martyrdom. The painting of *menologia* has its roots in the miniature illustration of manuscripts, particularly those of the 11th and 12th centuries. The inspiration and subjects of these icons are chiefly derived from the illuminated *menologia* of Symeon Metaphrastes (11th century) that have come from Constantinople. Some of the *menologia* have double inscriptions – both Greek and Iberian – betraying a close relation between the Monastery of Sinai and the monks or, more generally, the Church of Georgia.

«Sinaitic» icons

A large group of icons, dating from the 12th to the 15th century, consists of portrayals of personages associated with the Monastery because of the important role they played in the God-guided course of its history. These icons represent usually monks, abbots, patriarchs and Saints worshipped *par excellence* at Sinai, like the Virgin of the Burning Bush, the Prophet Moses, St. Catherine, St. John Climacus. Most of the icons must have been painted in the Monastery, and their varied style, technique and quality depend largely on the artistic skill of the painter. Some examples include a representation of the dedicant monk himself, kneeling, praying or making *proskynesis* before the Saint portrayed. These icons are an important source of information on the Monastery's history and art and on the general activity of notable personalities who lived in the Monastery of Sinai.

Icons of the 13th century and the Palaeologan age

A considerable number of icons is assigned to the 13th century, and an even greater number continues the tradition into the 14th and 15th centuries, i.e. the age of the Palaeologi. New artistic currents made their appearance in the 13th century, with a tendency to renovate elements of plasticity and revert to normal proportions in the treatment of masses. In fact, the 13th century prepared the ground for the art of the so-called Palaeologan Revival. Variety of style is a distinctive feature of this period, noticeable in icons from the hermitages of South Italy to the Venetian-ruled islands of the Aegean, and from the delicate technique of Constantinopolitan ateliers to the decorative character of Cypriot painting. All these tendencies were represented and assimilated in that remote outpost of Orthodoxy, the Monastery of Sinai. Outstanding among the large group of 13th century works is a fine double-sided icon, with the Sts. Sergius and Bacchus on horseback on one side and the Virgin Hodegetria on the other.

In the late Byzantine period (Palaeologan age) iconography no longer adhered to the established traditional standards. Icon-painters followed new currents and trends dominated by a more realistic treatment of figures and scenes. Their works are characterized by freedom of expression and variety of type, by novel subjects and many-figured compositions. Such works were to give rise to the art of the post-Byzantine period, particularly of the 16th century, by enriching the iconographic cycles and remaining open to influences from the art of the West and the Renaissance.

To this group belong «the Crucifixion bordered with scenes from the Dodecaorton and the Passion», «the Great Deesis with full-length Saints in successive rows», the icons of «Christ Pantocrator», «the Virgin Platytera enthroned», «the Virgin and Child», «the Archangels» etc.

Post-Byzantine Cretan icons

The Monastery of Sinai is known to have maintained a close and lasting contact with Crete, primarily through the Sinaitic Church of St. Catherine at Herakleion and later, in the years of the Turkish occupation, through the small Sinaitic Church of St. Matthew at Candia.

The existence to this day at Sinai of works by celebrated painters of the «Cretan School» is therefore hardly surprising. The Monastery's collection of Cretan icons includes works by Michael Damaskenos, Georgios Klontzas, Emmanuel Lampardos, Emmanuel Tzane - Bounialis Jeremias Palladas, Victor the Cretan, Georgios Kastrofy-lakas, Angelos the Cretan and Ioannes Kornaros. It is a splendid collection comprising representative examples of post-Byzantine icon-painting.

The mosaic of the Transfiguration

The sanctuary apse of the Monastery's church (Katholikon) is decorated with the magnificent mosaic of the Transfiguration. The subject is most appropriate to this holy site, which is associated with the two instances when God was «şeen»: by the Prophet Moses and by the Prophet Elijah (the latter had felt God as a light breeze on Mount Horeb, below the Peak of the Decalogue). Moreover, this has been *par excellence* the favourite subject of the monks who aspire to holiness, to become worthy of contemplating and viewing God's ineffable glory, the increate Taborian Light.

Christ is portrayed with black hair and beard in an oval «glory», between Moses and Elijah who represent the Law and the Prophets. Below, the three awed disciples are pictured in different poses. The soffit of the triumphal arch is decorated with medallions containing busts of the twelve Apostles. The three Apostles included in the scene of the Transfiguration have been replaced in the chain of medallions by Paul, Thaddaeus and Matthias. The base of the apse is bordered by another series of fifteen medallions with busts of the Prophets.

This monumental composition of the late 6th century is a true masterpiece of Byzantine art. Through this subject, treated with intense light and profound spirituality, the mosaicist has succeeded to represent in a most expressive and transcendental manner the doctrine of the two natures of Christ, as formulated in A.D. 451 by the Ecumenical Council of Chalcedon.

The terminal medallions enclose the portraits of Longinus the Abbot (right) and John the Deacon (left). Both were important personalities. Longinus was Abbot of the Monastery of Sinai in 562-565/6 – at which time the decoration was executed – and afterwards became Patriarch of Antioch. John is perhaps the later Patriarch of Jerusalem known as John IV (575-594).

The spandrels of the arch are occupied by two flying angels and the centre by the Amnos (Lamb). The Virgin is depicted in bust on the south side and St. John the Baptist on the north. We may say that we have here one of the earliest representations of the Deesis.

The upper part of the wall shows two episodes from the Old Testament: Moses before the Burning Bush not consumed by fire, and Moses receiving the Tablets of the Law.

This superb mosaic must have been made by master mosaicists who had come from Constantinople. Cleaning and conservation operations, undertaken in 1958 by American experts, revealed the brightness and delicacy of the colours, the lively treatment of the subject and the excellent quality of this unique work of art.

Because of the sanctity and spirituality of the site and the famous mosaic of the Transfiguration, the Monastery's Katholikon became known with the passing of centuries as «Church of the Transfiguration of Christ the Saviour». To this day it is known under this name, in addition to the original name in honour of the Virgin of the Burning Bush and the later one in honour of St. Catherine.

SINAI AND SAINT CATHERINE

Sinai became widely known, particularly in Europe, with the spreading of the fame and cult of St. Catherine. Symeon Metaphrastes contributed greatly in making the life of the Saint known to the laity when, in the 10th century, he wrote on «the martyrdom of the great Martyr and in the name of Christ victorious Saint Catherine».

The high-born learned maiden had studied at the ethnic schools of that age philosophy, rhetorics, poetry, music, physics, mathematics, astronomy and medicine. Her beauty and amazing learning, her aristocratic birth and noble character did not prevent her from accepting Jesus Christ, «the heavenly spouse», and she was baptized a Christian.

When in the beginning of the 4th century the emperor Maximinus persecuted the Christians, Catherine publicly accused the emperor of worshipping idols and fearlessly confessed her Christian faith. To dissuade her, the emperor ordered fifty philosophers to discuss with Catherine and demolish her Christian arguments. Their attempt failed, and they, along with many others from the emperor's closer circle, believed in Christ. When Maximinus realized the futility of these efforts, he resorted to torture. He gave orders for the making of spiked wheels, but even this horrible torment failed to break the Saint, who was finally beheaded. Her body was then taken by angels and carried to the highest peak of Mount Sinai.

St. Catherine's martyrdom and her relation to the Monastery of Sinai became known in the West when Symeon Metaphrastes brought relics of the Saint to Rouen and Trèves, in France. The fame of the Saint spread rapidly in Europe and the Monastery of Sinai came to be known as the Monastery of St. Catherine. Generous gifts were sent to Sinai and estates were donated to the Monastery by European countries. «No Saint was loved in the West more than St. Catherine». Master painters – like Fra Angelico, Correggio, Rubens, Titian and Murillo – immortalized on canvas scenes from the life and martyrdom of St. Catherine.

The Saint's cult and iconography had likewise spread in the East. She was portrayed in royal robes, wearing a crown and surrounded with objects alluding to her wisdom and martyrdom: a quill-pen, a globe, books, and a spiked wheel. To these the Byzantine hagiographers added depictions of Mount Sinai, Mount Horeb and the Mount of St. Catherine.

A great number of the Saint's icons, often bordered with miniature scenes from her life and martyrdom, are kept to this day in the Monastery.

The Saint's relics have been placed since early times in a marble chest. This *larnax* is mentioned in an itinerary dated 1231. In later years (1688) the royal family of Russia sent a silver casket, a gift of the Czars of Russia as recorded by the Cyrillic inscriptions, but the holy relics remained in the old marble chest.

From the late Byzantine age to the 20th century, whenever and wherever the Monastery of Sinai founded a *metochi* (dependency) it gave it the name of St. Catherine. The most active and famed Sinai Dependency of St. Catherine was the one at Herakleion in Crete, visited by numerous personalities of the Church, the arts and the letters.

BUILDINGS OF THE MONASTIC COMPOUND

Nine chapels are incorporated in the Monastery's Katholikon: the chapels of the Burning Bush, of St. James, of the Holy Fathers slain at Sinai and Raitho, of St. Marina, of Sts. Constantine and Helen, of St. Antypas, of Sts. Cosmas and Damian, of St. Symeon the Stylite and of St. Anne. There are twelve other chapels within the compound.

The *Chapel of the Burning Bush,* which is the most important one, is situated behind the sanctuary of the Katholikon. Aetheria, the 4th century pilgrim from Spain, has given a plain description of the locality and the shrine: «We had to advance deep into the valley for there are many hermit cells and a shrine at the site of the Bush. The Bush is verdant to this day. This is the Bush of which I have spoken earlier, the one from which God in a flame of fire spoke to Moses. The Bush is in a very beautiful garden in front of the church». The pilgrim enters the chapel barefooted in remembrance of God's command to Moses *«put off thy shoes from off thy feet...».* The Chapel of the Burning Bush honours the Annunciation to the Holy Virgin. The iconographical type of «the Virgin of the Burning Bush» represents the Mother of Christ seated within the Burning Bush and holding her Son, with Moses worshipping barefooted on the left. A mosaic cross of the 10th century decorates the apse of the chapel. Divine Service is celebrated every Saturday.

The present *bell-tower* was built in 1871 and the cost defrayed by Father Gregory, then sacristan of the Monastery. The nine bells are a gift of the Czars of Russia and are rung for Services on Sundays and feast-days, whereas the wooden *semantron* (also known as *talanton*) is struck for Vespers and Matins.

The *Old Refectory* is an oblong hall with pointed Gothic arches preserving stone carvings with Frankish inscriptions and coats-of-arms. The small conch is decorated with a 16th century painting showing the Hospitality of Abraham, in which the three angels symbolize the Holy Trinity. A monumental composition of the Last Judgement covers the entire surface of the wall. The long narrow wooden dining-table, placed in the middle of the hall, was made and carved in Corfu, in the 17th century.

The *Gallery of Icons* comprises a small but select part of the Monastery's vast collection. From the almost 2,000 icons, which form an inestimable cultural heritage covering 15 centuries, 90 were chosen for their unique artistic value and are exhibited in this icon gallery, in the narthex of the Katholikon. They represent in an historic and stylistic sequence all the trends and techniques of Byzantine art. The Gallery's collection includes encaustic icons from the 6th to the 10th century, Greek, Georgian, Syrian, Coptic; Byzantine icons from the 11th to the 15th century; icons of the 16th century; other icons representative of the Cretan School and of later post-Byzantine art.

Drawing by the architect Christos Katsibinis

SINA 10.75

Drawing by the architect Christos Katsibinis

31

The *Library* is considered one of the largest and most important in the world. It contains a rich collection of 4,500 manuscripts, mainly Greek but also Arabic, Syriac, Egyptian, Slavonic etc. The regrettable story of one of the most precious manuscripts in the world, the *Codex Sinaiticus,* is well known. This mid-4th century Greek text of the Holy Scriptures was officially borrowed in 1859 by the German scholar K. van Tischendorf on behalf of the Czar of Russia, but it was never returned. In 1933, it was purchased by the British Museum where it is kept to this day.

Many of the manuscripts are illuminated with rare and fine miniatures. In addition to the manuscripts, the Library contains a considerable number of printed books. About 5,000 are old editions, some of which dating from the early days of the art of printing. The Library has been organized in a scientific method and is equipped with laboratories for the conservation and the microfilming of manuscripts. Both the Library and its archives are at the disposal of scholars engaged in special studies.

The *garden and orchard* outside the Monastery's enclosure is a true oasis in the desolate landscape of granite rock. Aetheria mentions in her itinerary a very pleasant garden with plenty of water near the Burning Bush. Other pilgrims and writers also refer to this garden in later times. Today, vegetables, fruit-trees, decorative plants and flowers are grown on soil that the monks have carried at times from distant places. Water from the rains and the melting snow is collected in huge cisterns and used to irrigate the garden and orchard.

In the garden is the small *cemetery* with the Chapel of St. Tryphon and the Charnel House. The scantiness of earth does not permit permanent graves – the monks buried in the cemetery are later exhumed and their bones placed in the ossuary. The Charnel House also serves a spiritual purpose: the sight of the piled bones makes both monks and visitors meditate on life and death, on the vanity of human and earthly matters.

Under a canopy sits the cadaver of St. Stephanos the hermit, a 6th century monk mentioned by St. John Climacus.

PLACES OF PILGRIMAGE OUTSIDE THE MONASTERY

A long flight of 3,700 steps leads to the *Peak of Mount Sinai.* A church was built on this site quite early, possibly in the 4th century, and rebuilt later under Justinian on plans by the architect Stephanos of Aila. The Justinianic church, now preserved to the height of the foundations, was fairly large, measuring 21 m. in length and 11.50 m. in width. A mosque was built later on the mountain peak. Some fifty years ago (in 1933), a small chapel dedicated to the Holy Trinity was raised over part of the ruins of Justinian's church.

Mount Horeb is of special importance by reason of the «Peak of the Decalogue». A church consecrated to the Prophet Elijah was built on this peak. Ephraim the Deacon records the existence of twelve chapels on the slopes and summit of Mount Horeb.

A chapel dedicated to St. Catherine stands on the *Mount of St. Catherine,* at the site where the Saint's body was found. Opposite the Monastery, on the *Mount of St. Episteme,* are a hermitage and a chapel in this Saint's name and also a cave in the name of St. Galaktion.

A chapel consecrated to the Sts. Theodoroi stands on the *Hill of Jethro* and a small church on the *Hill of Aaron.* In the *Valley of the Forty Martyrs* is preserved the chapel of the Holy Apostles and at the locality known as «Bustan» the chapel honouring the Birth of the Virgin. Other shrines are the Monastery's Dependency of the Forty Martyrs and, in the garden, the chapel of St. Onouphrios.

In the well-known *Valley of Thola* are preserved to this day a cave and chapel that were the retreat of the celebrated St. John Scholasticus, also known as St. John Climacus after his renowned work. In the same area is the Monastery's Dependency of the Sts. Anargyroi.

The small *Valley of Faran* had the privilege of being the See of the first Bishopric of the Sinai Peninsula. The latest excavations at Faran have brought to light the foundations, the floor and a ruined wall of the ancient church and annexes.

Raitho (the present-day El-Tor) is one of the most famed places. It is here that in the time of the Roman emperor Diocletian the Holy Fathers of Sinai were massacred by the Blemmyes of Africa. A letter addressed by the Abbot John, *Hegoumenos* of Raitho, to «John the most worthy *Hegoumenos* of Mount Sinai» has survived. From this we learn that at the time of the Abbot John there was a *lavra* (group of hermit dwellings) at Raitho. The *Hegoumenos* of Sinai was asked to give advice to the monks of the *lavra* at Raitho, and this is how the God-inspired monastic work *Ladder to Heaven* was composed. The number of manuscripts of the *Ladder to Heaven* preserved in the Monastery of Sinai (nos. 416-430) is remarkable. Equally remarkable are the translations of this work into «simple Greek» and its many versions, of which the most notable is that by Maximus Margunius.

Among the valleys we should also mention: the *Valley of Ramhan,* in which the *lavra* of St. Arselaus and the *cathisma* (small monastic habitation with chapel) of St. Antony were located; the *Valley of El-Hodra,* where there is a rock with various inscriptions; and the so-called *Valley of Mukhattab,* i.e. Valley of Inscriptions.

Men of great virtue and fame had lived at times in these regions. Teaching in the wilderness they glorified the desert, and their inspired writings proclaimed the profound truth of Orthodoxy to the whole world.

THE BEDOUINS

The Bedouins of Sinai belong to the local Arab tribe known as *Djebeliyeh* (= mountaineer) and have lived for centuries under the shelter of the Monastery. They are Moslems but honour the Prophet Moses on the Holy Peak and venerate St. George and St. Catherine. They have special duties in serving the Monastery.

A number of written sources refer to the origin of the Bedouins. Eutychios,

Patriarch of Alexandria, writes in the 9th century that the emperor Justinian ordered 200 families from Pontus and Alexandria to Sinai, to work in the service of the monks.

Today, in our mechanized age, when the distance from Cairo to the Monastery of Sinai is covered in 6 hours by a regular coach service, the pilgrim will seldom see Bedouins with their nonchalantly stepping camels, treading the stony pathways of the desert under the scorching sun. Even more rare is an encounter with a whole family of wandering Bedouins or the sight of Bedouin tents pitched in the Oasis of Faran.

Inside the Monastery, during the hours of silence, the pilgrim in the shade of the Katholikon and the scholar in the Library may turn their minds and meditate upon the centuries that have rolled by, outside the Monastery's walls. But, within the enclosure, time has another dimension and those living here are at all times prepared to meet with the ecstatic Moses, see the Bush that burned with fire but was not consumed, behold the angels carrying the body of St. Catherine, listen to the steps of St. John Climacus climbing one by one the rungs of the «Ladder to Heaven», bow and kiss the holy ground on which God had walked and feel the breath of eternity in the very depth of their souls. For here, on this «God-trodden» mountain of Sinai, the Eternal and the Divine have met with the temporary and the human.

1. *The Sinai Peninsula with part of Egypt and of Saudi Arabia, as photographed by an American satellite. The original slide has been made available by courtesy of the NASA.*

2. *Detailed map of the Sinai Peninsula.*

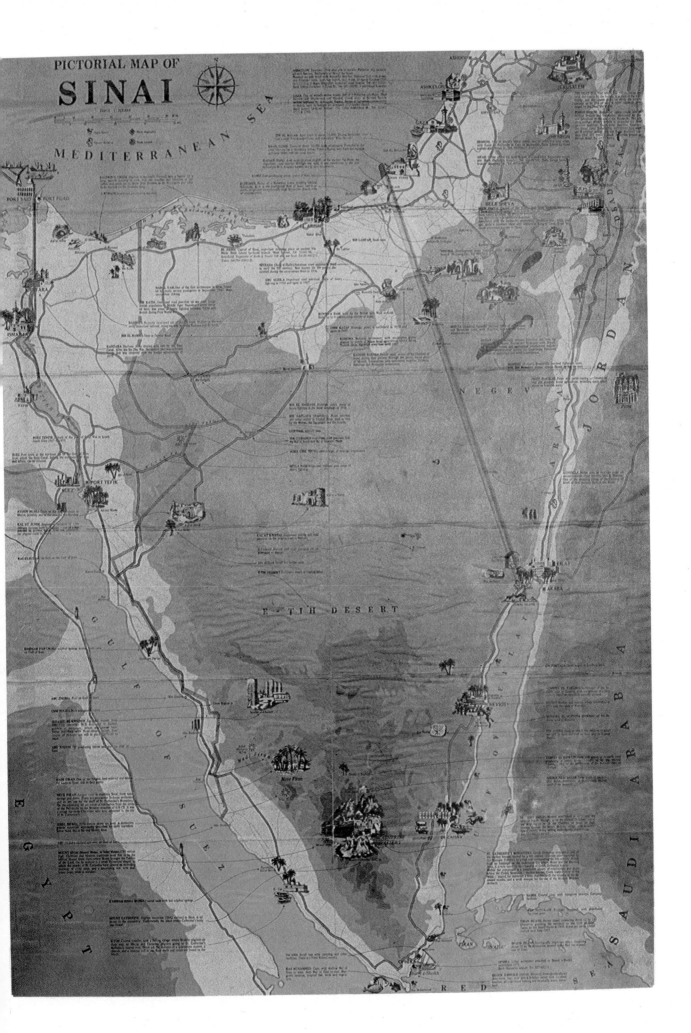

3. Inland scenery of the Sinai Peninsula on the way to St. Catherine's Monastery.

3

4. Building on a hillock near the small coastal town of Abu-Zuneima.

4

5

5. The exit from the Ahmad Hamdi Tunnel with signposts indicating the way to Sinai.

6. *The entrance to the tunnel recently constructed under the Suez Canal. A wonder of engineering inaugurated in 1980, the Ahmad Hamdi Tunnel runs 37 m. below sea level to a length of 1,700 m., connecting the Sinai Peninsula with the rest of the Egyptian territory.*

6

7. *Inside the tunnel.*

7

8

8. *The Suez Canal.*

9. *Magnificent Sinaitic landscape near the El-Gharandel Pass.*

9

10. *Plantation of date-palms near El-Tor, the ancient Raitho.*

11. The Gulf of Aqabah.
    View from the eastern
    coast of the Sinai
    Peninsula.

12. Islet in the Gulf of Aqa-
    bah, covered with
    ruined buildings of
    various periods
    including an ancient
    monastery.

11

14

13. View of the eastern coast of the Sinai Peninsula and the Gulf of Aqabah.

14. Gulf of Aqabah. Granite rocks with coral formations on the eastern coast of the Sinai Peninsula.

15. *Bedouin riding a camel, the traditional form of transport now usually replaced by an old jeep.*

16. *Young Bedouin girl gracefully covering her face from the photographer's camera.*

15

17. *Bedouin carrying a load of* ghassum *(dry bushes growing on granite rocks) to be used as fuel against the* winter cold.

17

18

18. *A monk standing on the rippling sand near Abu-Rodeis.*

19. *A Bedouin in the Valley of Faran.*

20. *Tent housing a Bedouin family in the vicinity of the Monastery of Sinai.*

21. *Characteristic type of a Bedouin woman.*

22. *Young Bedouin girl sitting outside her tent.*

19

20

21

22

23

23. Below the Peak of [Moses], near the Chapel [of] the Prophet Elijah, [two] Bedouins and a m[onk] of the Monastery [are] drinking a cup of c[offee] fee after some h[ard] work at the chapel.

24

24. Scene from a Bedo[uin] wedding celebrati[on]. Boiled goat's meat [is] cut into pieces to [be] offered to the men a[nd] women guests sitt[ing] separately in the sha[de] of the tent.

25

25. Another scene from t[he] same wedding feast.

20. Traditional scene from the life of the Sinai Bedouins. Tents are now being replaced by small dwellings built of stone.

27. *Camel-race between Bedouins on the occasion of a wedding feast.*

28. *Two monks walking towards the hermitage known as «Daniel's Cell», near the chapels of the Prophets Elijah and Elisha on Mount Horeb, below the Peak of Moses.*

27

29. General view of St. Catherine's Monastery at Sinai, from the northeast.

30. General view of the monastic complex at the foot of Mount Horeb, including the newly-built hostel with part of the garden and orchard.

31. North view of the monastic complex.

32

33

34

35

32. 34. 35. Early Christian cross symbols carved in relief on the granite blocks of the south side of the Justinian wall enclosing the Monastery.

33. Inscription of later date on the Justinian wall by the entrance to the Monastery.

36. *The south wall of the 6th century fortified enclosure of the Monastery with parts showing repairs of later date.*

36

37. *Night view of the Monastery from the northeast including the new hostel and the garden.*

38. Night view of the hostel for official visitors.

39. General view of the Monastery at night. The building with the arcaded galleries houses the Library and the monks' quarters.

39

38

40

40. Night view of the Chapel of the Timios Prodromos within the monastic compound.

41. Night view. In the foreground, an arch of Justinian's period; in the background, to the left, the Well of Moses, by which the Prophet delivered Jethro's daughters out of the hands of the shepherds (Ex. 2, 15-19).

41

42. The ancient Well of Moses (now equipped with a hand-operated water pump), by which the Prophet met the daughters of Jethro (Ex. 2, 15-19) (see also Pl. 41).

43. Partial view of the interior of the Monastery. The staircase to the left leads to the Chapel of the Zoodochos Pege.

44. Façade of the three-aisled basilica (the Monastery's Katholikon) with the bell-tower of later date.

45. Cross between date-palms, carved in relief on the granite pediment of the three-aisled basilica.

46. The plant of the Bush that «burned with fire and was not consumed» (Ex. 3, 2).

45

46

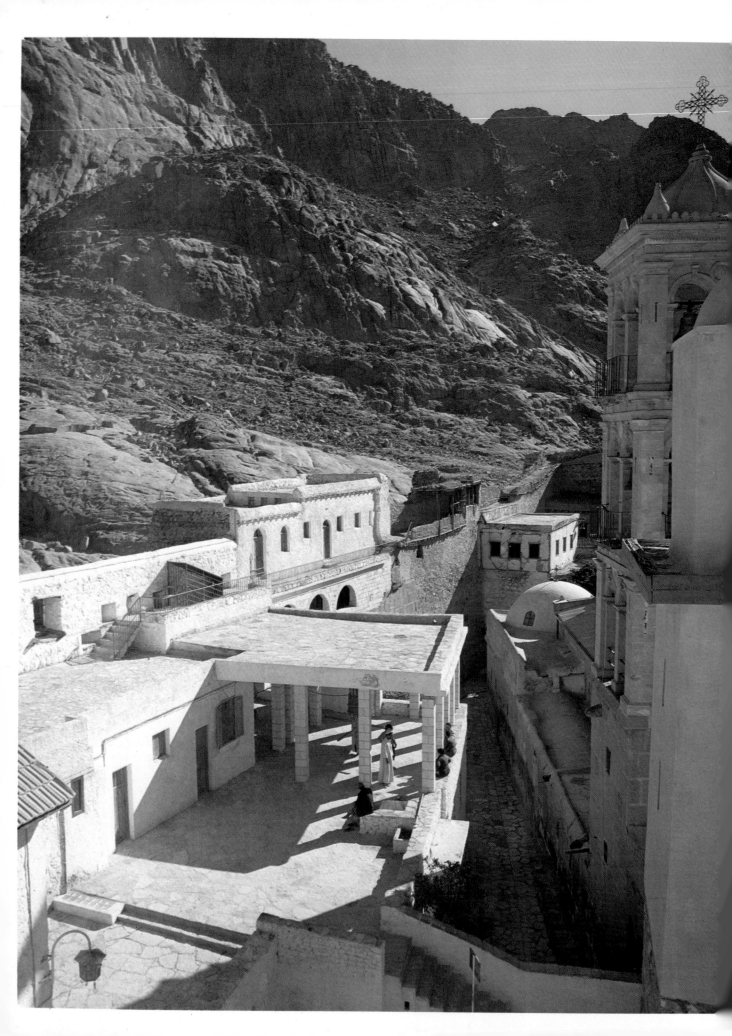

47. North view of the Monastery showing part of the Katholikon and, in the foreground, the bell-tower of the church and the minaret of the ancient mosque. The Chapel of St. George can be seen on the north wall.

48. Exterior view of the east side of the Katholikon. The foliage of the Burning Bush «not consumed by fire» can be seen in the foreground, outside the church.

48

49. *Extensive interior view of the Monastery.*

50. *Interior view of the Monastery. The arcaded passages lead from the entrance to the Monastery's Church (Katholikon).*

51. *Interior view of the Monastery. Entrance to the Library.*

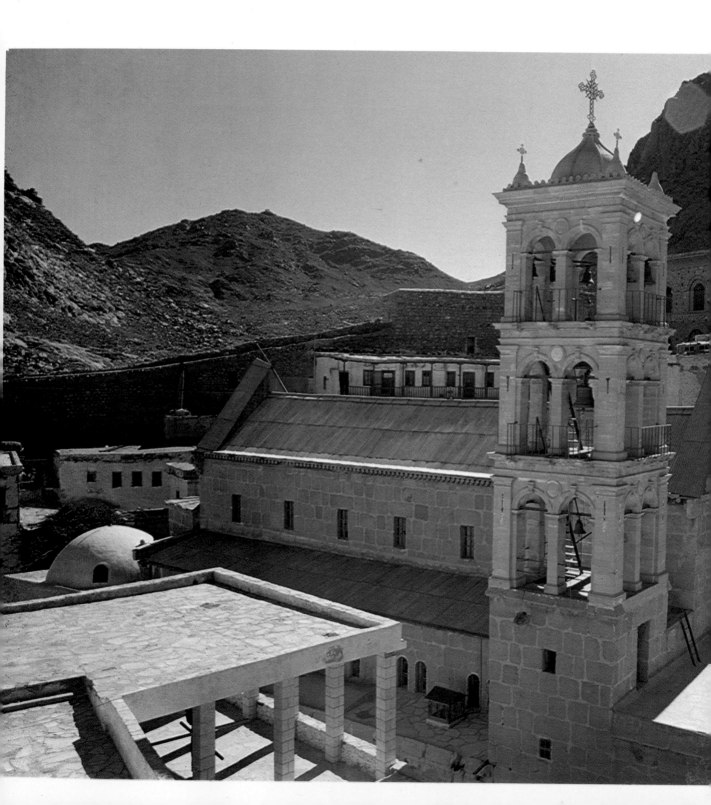

49　50

51

52   53

52. North section of the Monastery's Wall by the Katholikon. The passageway leads to the plant of the Burning Bush, located to the right behind the Church.

53. Double-arched window of the Justinian age in the south wall of the narthex of the Katholikon.

54. Part of the old compound of cells used by the monks.

55. A monk strikes the «mallet» against the wooden semantron for Vespers in the Monastery.

58

56

57

56. 57. 59. *Views of the interior of the monastic complex from various angles.*

58. *View of the building housing the Library. Photograph taken from an opening of the double south wall, which forms an inner passageway.*

60. *Flight of steps leading to the entrance of the Monastery's Church.*

61. *Facade of the Chapel of St. John the Theologian.*

59

60   61

62

62. *A monk striking the* talanton, *calling the monks to Vespers.*

63. *The monk acting as* ekklesares *(sexton), sweeping away a thin layer of snow from the roof of the narthex of the Monastery's Church.*

64. *Interior of the old Refectory of the Monastery before its recent restoration. The arches show inscriptions and emblems from the age of the Crusades. The wooden dining-table is of the 16th - 17th century.*

63

65

66

65. Entrance to the narthex of
    Katholikon. The tympan[
    under the granite arch
    painted with a representat[
    of the Transfiguration of la[
    date.

66. Detail of the 12th century p[
    tal of carved wood giving a[
    cess into the narthex.

67. The wooden triple door to [
    narthex dating from the 1[
    century. To protect it, a gla[
    door was added at a mu[
    later date.

68. Interior of the Monastery's Katholikon. The splendid three-aisled basilica dates from the 6th century but the interior decoration is of later date. The icon-screen of Cretan art dates from 1612 and was made in the Monastery's Dependency of Candia (Herakleion) in Crete.

69. From the Holy Services conducted in the Katholikon. The Bishop incensing during Vespers of the Easter Agape.

70. Conducting the Divine Service in front of the Holy Table, under the superb 6th century mosaic of the Transfiguration.

71. Similar scene with the Bishop preceded by the Deacon carrying the triple-candle (trikeron).

72. Lighting large candles during Vespers.

73. Procession of prelates co-celebrating Vespers in the Katholikon of the Monastery.

69

74

The doorway leading from the narthex to the naos of the Monastery's Katholikon. The wooden double folding doors, carved and decorated with animal and floral motifs, have been in use since the 6th century and are preserved in excellent condition. The phiale for the blessing of water and the icon-stand are also visible.

Panel of the 6th century wooden doors leading from the narthex to the naos of the Katholikon.

. The middle iron-bound door of the entrance to the Monastery, dating from the 16th century.

78 79

*. The inner iron-bound door of the entrance, also dating from the 16th century.

*. Detail of the metal casket (Pl. 80) with a relief representation of two angels carrying the body of St. Catherine.

*. Detail of the relief representation of St. Catherine on the metal casket (Pl. 80).

*. Metal casket with relief representation of St. Catherine, presented to the Monastery by a Russian Princess in 1860, to contain the Saint's holy relics. These, however, were left in the older marble chest placed within the sanctuary, behind the icon-screen.

31. 17th century portable icon of St. Catherine with scenes from the Saint's life and martyrdom.

+ΕΓΕΝ
ΕΤΟΔΕ
ΤΗΗΜ
ΕΡΑΤΗ
ΤΡΙΤΗ
ΓΕΝΗ
ΘΕΝΤ
ΟCΠΡ
ΟCΟΡ
ΘΡΟΝ
ΕΓΙΝ
ΟΝΤ
ΟΦΟ
ΝΕΚ
ΑCΤ
ΡΑΠΕ
ΚΑΙ ΠΑΡΕCΤΗCΑΝ ΥΠΟ ΤΟ ΟΡΟC ΤΟ CΙΝΑ
ΤΑCΑΕΚΤΩΝCΩΝCΟΙΠΡΟCΦΕΡΟΜΕΝΚΕ

82. Large bronze cross of the Early Christian period, probably of the 6th century, inscribed with the passage from Exodus describing how God delivered the Ten Commandments to Moses on Mount Sinai.

83. Small reliquary with bones of various Saints, placed within the sanctuary.

84. Another large metal casket kept in the sanctuary. The relief decoration by Russian artists of the 17th century includes a representation of St. Catherine. The names of the donors appear in Russian on the sides of the casket.

83

84

85. The distinctive insignia of the episcopal office and the abbot's staff, used by the Archbishop of Sinai in his function as Hegoumenos of the Monastery of Sinai, also called Monastery of St. Catherine.

86. The Holy Table in the conch of the sanctuary of the small Chapel of the Burning Bush, located behind the apse of the Katholikon. The chapel is consecrated to the Holy Virgin (as the Bush not consumed by the fire of God). A Divine Service is held every Saturday and all enter the chapel barefooted in remembrance of the Lord's word who said unto Moses «put off thy shoes from off thy feet, for the place whereon thou standest is holy ground» (Ex. 3, 5).

87. *Ceremonial silver paten for the rite of* artoklasia *(Breaking of Bread) with remarkable representations of events related to Sinai. 17th century.*

Three woodcarved crosses in silver filigree frames set with precious stones. 16th-18th century.

90

Book of extracts
from the Gospels
to be read during
the Divine Liturgy.
It has gold and
silver relief
ornaments and
enamel portrayals
of the Resurrection
and of the four
Evangelists. 18th
century.

Large chalice
decorated with
enamel and
precious stones.
18th century.

91. *Cross embroidered on cloth, showing Christ in the centre and the four Evangelists on the arms. 17th century.*

92. *Ceremonial cloth-cover for the reliquary of St. Catherine with fine embroidered scenes from the Saint's life. The central representation shows the angels carrying the Saint's body to the highest peak of Mount Sinai. 17th century.*

93. *Part of an embroidered large episcopal stole (omophorion). 18th century.*

92

91

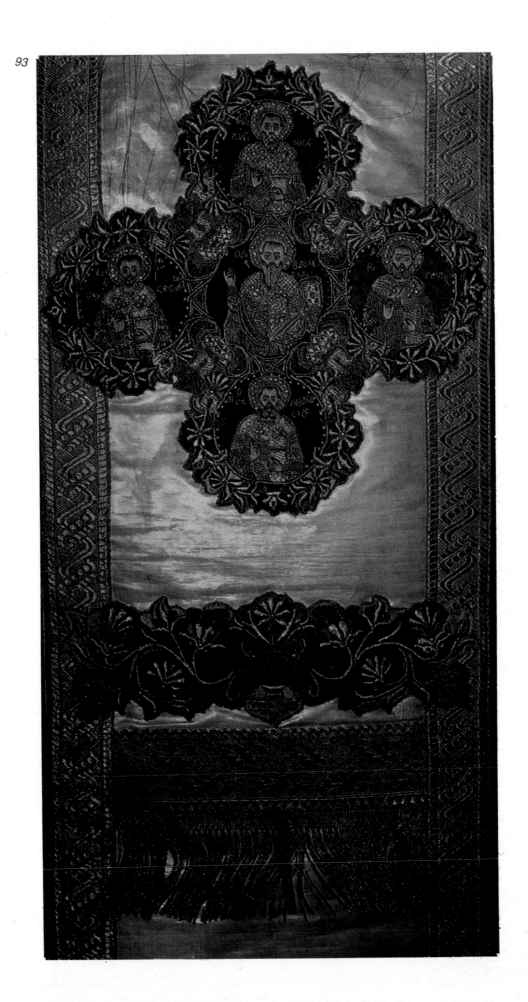

94. *All-embroidered archpriest's chasuble (sakkos) of outstanding workmanship. 18th century. One side shows the Tree of Jesse illustrating the genealogy of the Holy Virgin and of our Lord Jesus Christ. The other side shows Christ as High Priest and the twelve Apostles, with God the Father and the Holy Spirit «consenting» above the figure of Christ.*

95. *The same chasuble from the side embroidered with the Tree of Jesse showing the genealogy of David, the Virgin Mary and Jesus Christ.*

95

96. *The magnificent, excellently preserved, 6th century mosaic of the Transfiguration in the sanctuary apse of the Katholikon. The scene is bordered by a chain of medallions with portraits of the sixteen Prophets and of the Prophet King David (in the centre) at the base of the apsidal arch, and of the twelve Apostles on the soffit of the aspidal arch. The theme of the Transfiguration, i.e. the Taborian Light and the Glory of God, is the highest aspiration and supreme goal of life in accordance with the teachings of Christ, attainable through the ideal of monasticism.*

97. *Central detail of the mosaic of the Transfiguration. The successive elliptical circles of different shades composing the mandorla surrounding the figure of Christ indicate the supernatural light emitted by the theanthropic nature of the Lord, which dazzled the ecstatic disciples, Sts. Peter, James and John.*

96

97

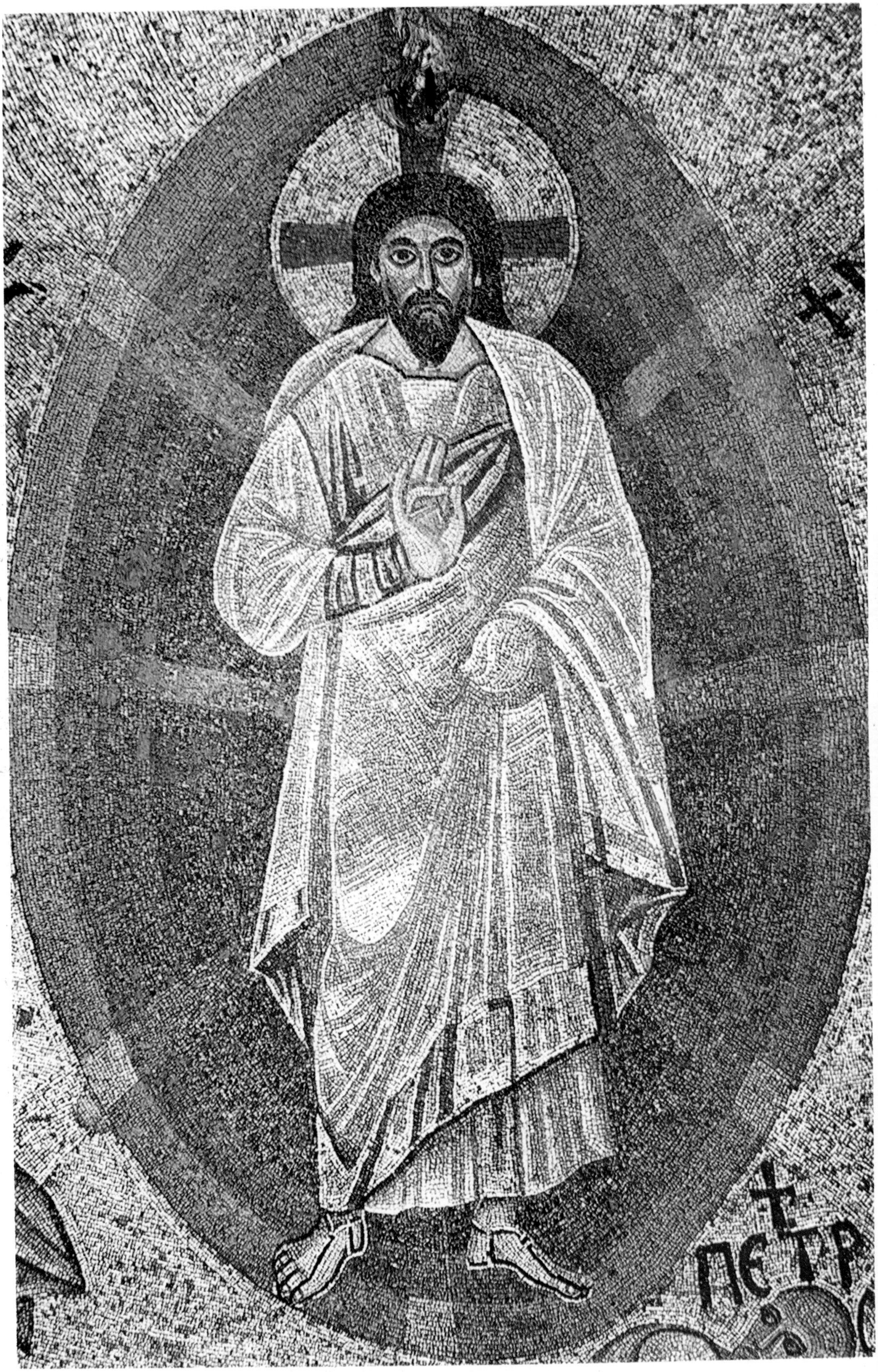

8. Detail of Pl. 99, showing the head of Christ. The ecstatic expression of the face with the raised eyebrow is considered unique.

9. Christ Pantocrator. Portable icon in the encaustic technique, of outstanding artistic quality. 7th century.

102. *The Sacrifice of Jephthah's Daughter. Encaustic painting on marble decorating the right pilaster of the sanctuary apse. 6th century*

103. *Abraham sacrificing his son Isaac. Representation painted in the encaustic technique, on the marble revetment of the left pilaster supporting the apse of the sanctuary in the Monastery's Katholikon.*

104. *St. Peter the Apostle. The roundels above the Saint's figure enclose portraits of Christ (in the centre), the Virgin and another Saint, possibly St. John the Evangelist. A splendid icon in the encaustic technique. 6th century.*

102

103

105. Hagiologion, *calendar icon presenting all the Saints in the order of their feast day within a year. Portable diptych of the 13th century.*

106. *The Crucifixion in a frame containing busts of Saints. Portable icon of high artistic quality. 12th century.*

106

107. *The Virgin of the Passion. Portable icon of the 16th century.*

108. *The Nativity and related scenes. Middle panel of a 13th century triptych icon.*

109. *St. Catherine enthroned with the symbols of her wisdom and martyrdom. Small portable icon painted on a sizeable shell from the Red Sea.*

109

110

111

112

St. Catherine. Portable icon of later style placed on an icon-stand.

St. Catherine, a large portable icon of Spanish art. 15th century.

St. Catherine enthroned with the symbols of her wisdom and martyrdom. Portable icon of the 17th century.

St. Catherine enthroned with the symbols of her wisdom and martyrdom. 16th century icon on the iconostasis of the Monastery's Katholikon.

114

114. The Annunciation,
the cycle of the
Feasts (Dodecaort
an iconostasis
12th century.

115. The Raising of La
from the Twelve
on the iconostasis
12th century.

116. The Miracle at C
portable icon of hi
quality. 11th - 12th

115

Η ΕΓΕΡCIC ΤΥ ΛΑΖΑΡΥ

117

117. The Entry into Jerusal[...] from the Twelve Fea[...] on an iconostasis be[...] 12th century.

118. The Transfiguration, fro[...] Twelve Feasts on the [...] stasis beam. 12th cent[...]

119. The Baptism, from [...] Twelve Feasts on the i[...] stasis beam. 12th cent[...]

118

120. *The Archangels Michael and Gabriel, a remarkable portable icon. 12th - 13th century.*

121. *The Archangel Michael in attitude of prayer. Portable icon of Cretan art. 16th century.*

121

122. The Archangel Gabriel. Detail of the Annunciation from the Twelve Feasts cycle on the iconostasis beam. 12th century.

123. The body of St. Catherine being carried by angels to the highest peak of Mount Sinai, after the Saint's glorious martyrdom. Detail of a 16th century portable icon in triptych form.

124. The Archangel Michael with the prostrated figure of the dedicant monk at his feet. Portable icon of the 12th century.

122

123

125. *Sts. Sergius and Bacchus. Detail of Pl. 126.*

126. *The two military Saints Sergius and Bacchus on horseback. Large portable icon of the 13th century.*

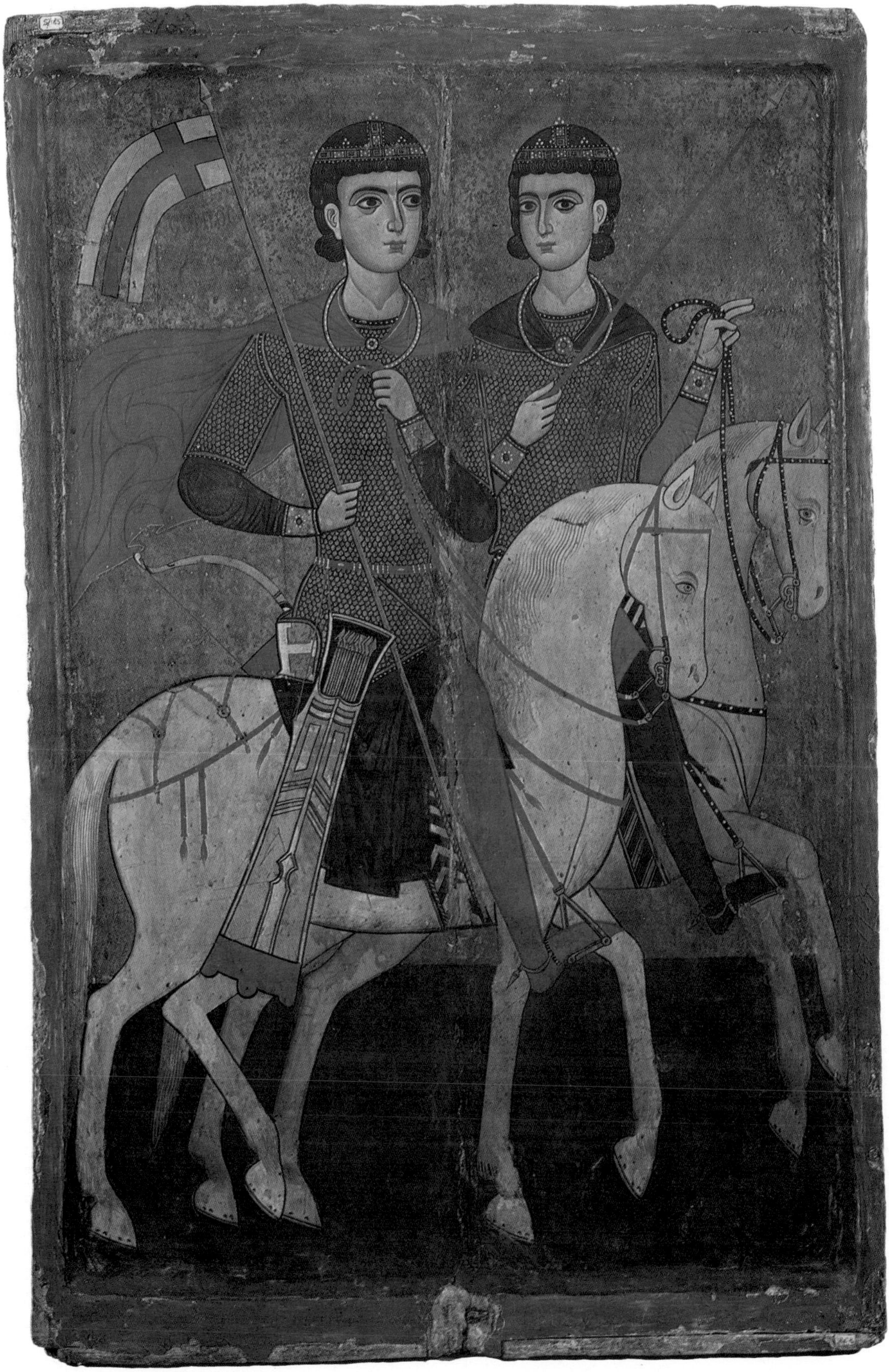

127. *St. Theodosia, portable icon of the 13th century.*

128. *St. Paul the Apostle, portable icon of the 16th century.*

129. *A unique portrait painting of St. George. Portable icon of the 13th century.*

128

127

129

130. Portable diptych icon showing four scenes from the life of Christ: the Annunciation, the Nativity, the Entry into Jerusalem and the Crucifixion. 12th - 13th century.

130

131

131. *A representation of the Monastery and of Mount Sinai on the Bishop's throne. 18th century.*

132. *Topographical icon of Mount Sinai showing St. Catherine's Monastery, various small convents and monastic habitations with chapels, as well as a reconstruction of the holy events related to the site. Portable icon of the 17th century.*

The Crucifixion surrounded with scenes from the life of Christ. Small portable icon of the 12th - 13th century.

The Prophet Moses on a panel of the sanctuary door. Cretan painting of the 17th century.

135. The theoptes *(i.e. one who looked upon God)* Prophet Moses receiving the Decalogue. Large portable icon of the 12th - 13th century.

136. The martyr St. Paraskeve carrying her severed head and surrounded with scenes from her martyrdom. Portable icon of the 18th century.

136

135

137

The theoptes *Prophet Moses receiving the Law from the Lord's hand. Portable icon of the 12th century.*

The *Apostles Paul, Andrew and Peter. Portable icon of the 13th - 14th century.*

138

139. *Deesis, the central scene in the Twelve Feasts cycle on the iconostasis beam. 12th century.*

140. *Three Saints (?). Portable icon of the 13th century.*

141. *The Ascension, a portable icon in the encaustic technique. 6th century.*

143. *The Anastasis and the Ascension, two scenes from the Twelve Feasts cycle on the iconostasis beam. 13th century.*

142. *The Presentation of Christ in the Temple, from the Twelve Feasts on the iconostasis beam. 12th century.*

142

143

145

144. The «Ladder to Heaven», representation inspired from the ascetic work of that name by St. John of Sinai known as St. John Climacus. Portable icon of the 12th - 13th century.

145. Great Deesis with Angels, Hierarchs, Martyrs, Hosioi and crowned Saints, grouped in five respective rows. Portable icon of the 12th century.

146. Christi enthroned in glo
Enamel on metal plate
13th century work of a

147. The Virgin Hodege
holding the Christ Cl
in her right arm. A 1
portable mosaic icon
the 13th century.

146

147

148. *The Monastery's Library. It contains about 3,200 catalogued manuscripts and another 1,100 manuscripts found lately, which are being catalogued at present.*

149. *A copy of the so-called* ahtiname, *i.e. the document granted by Mohammed the Founder of Islam to the Fathers of the Monastery, exhorting to respect and honour towards the Monks of the Sinai Desert.*

150

150. The beginning of the Sinai Codex 339, of parchment, in
Greek, 11th - 12th century. Left: St. Gregory the
Theologian writing. Right: The beginning of the Homily
«On the Holy Easter» with a representation of the
Anastasis.

† ΤΟΥ ΕΝ ΑΓΙΟΙΣ ΠΡ͞Σ ΗΜΩΝ ΓΡΗΓΟΡΙΟΥ ΤΟΥ ΘΕΟΛΟ
ΓΟΥ ΛΟΓΟΣ ΕΙΣ ΤΟΝ Τ͞ΕΣΧΑ͞ΚΑΙ ΕΙΣ ΤΗΝ ΒΡΑΔΥΤΗ͞Τ͞Α

ναστάσεως   Καὶ λαμπρω῾μ.
τρα. καὶ   θεωμ τοῦ ῾πᾶς
ἀρχ͞η. δόξιαῦ.   μηγύρει. καὶ λι͞.

5

151

152

151. *St. Luke the Evangelist (?) writing. Miniature illustration from a Sinaitic parchment manuscript containing extracts from the Gospels. 13th century.*

152. *St. Matthew the Evangelist (?). Miniature illustration from the same Sinaitic manuscript.*

153. *St. Gregory the Theologian writing. Full-page miniature illustration of excellent artistic quality from the Sinai Codex 339 (see Pl. 150).*

154. Illumination from the 11th century parchment manuscript No. 179 of the Monastery's Library.

155. Illuminated page from the 11th century parchment manuscript No. 275 of the Monastery's Library.

The Descent into Hell (Anastasis), from the illuminated Sinai Codex 339. Miniature illustration above the beginning of St. Gregory the Theologian's Homily «On the Holy Easter».

157. Illumination from a 17th ce[ntury]
liturgical manuscript conta[ining]
the Liturgy of St. John Ch[ryso]-
stom.

158. The prayer before the Grea[t En]-
troit is accompanied b[y a]
miniature illustration sho[wing]
angels carrying the Body o[f the]
Lord – «This is my body w[hich]
is given for you».

159. St. Gregory the Theolo[gian]
teaching the crowds. Mini[ature]
illustration above the begin[ning]
of the Homily «On Charity»[.]
Sinai Codex 339.

† ΤΟΥ ΑΥΤΟΥ ΠΕΡΙ ΦΙΛΟΠΤΩΧΙΑΣ ·†

ἄνδρες ἀδελφοὶ
καὶ συμπτωχοὶ μη
τῶ· πτωχοι εἰδρ
ἅπαντες λα
τῆς θείας χα
ριτος ἐν οὐδεὶς·
ἐὰν ἄλλος ἄλ
λου προσέχειν

δοκῶ μετ ροις
μετρος μετρου
μβρος, δοξασω
τὸν περὶ φιλο
πτωχιας λόγο·
μὴ ἀπωμι χερος,
ἀλλ ἀ φιλοτι
μος· ἱμαινα

160. *Miniature illustration from the 11th century Sinai Codex 1186, of parchment, in Greek. The scene shows the Sacrifice of Isaac.*

161-162. *Miniature illustration from Sinai Codex 1186, with scenes from the Exodus of the people of Israel, out of the bondage of the Pharaohs and towards the Promised Land across the Sinai desert.*

163. Christ seated in glory, according to the vision of the Prophet Habakkuk, with St. Gregory the Theologian praying to the left. Miniature illustration from the magnificent Sinai Codex 339, appearing above the Saint's Homily entitled «Another (Sermon) on the Holy Easter».

164. *Scenes from the Exodus: Moses before the Burning Bush, Moses receiving the Tablets of the Law, and th| People of Israel. Miniature illustration from Sinai Codex 1186.*

165. *The Ark of the Covenant with cherubim above and the Prophets Aaron and Moses on either side. Miniatu| illustration from Sinai Codex 1186.*

166. *Miniature illustration from the 11th century Sinai Codex 1186, showing Moses keeping his flock, picture| before the Burning Bush and receiving the Decalogue.*

167. *Pastoral scene. Decorative miniature at the beginning of a paragraph, from a parchment manuscript of th| 11th century.*

164

165

166   167

168. *Anchorite retiring in the desert. Miniature illustration in the chapter «On living abroad» from the ascetic work «Ladder to Heaven» by St. John of Sinai known as St. John Climacus. The miniature is from the 11th century parchment manuscript 418 of the Sinai Library.*

169. *The well-known, 5th century palimpsest Codex of the Sinai Library, in Syriac, with the second writing datable in about the 7th century.*

در کتاب مبارک التجارب که نسخهٔ ذیل تجارب الامم است از تصنیف ابن فندق

بیهقی و در جوامع العلوم از تصنیف اوری که بنام سلطان تکش است در فصل

تاریخ مذکور است که ملکا کین یکی بود از ارکان ملکت سلجوقیان چنانکه در مملکت

سامانیان الب تکین صاحب جیش خراسان از غرجستان غلامی تک خریده بود

نام او نوشتکین غرجه بود بتدریج بسبب عقل و کیاست منزلت مرتبتی یافت تا

بجای کهریشی بزرگ رسید و در دولت سلجوقیان مشابه ستکین بود و در آخر عهد ملوک

سامانی بسمت طشت داری داشت و خوارزم در ان وزکار در عدا وظیفه طشت

خانه بود چنانکه خورستان در وظیفه جامه خانه او را بسم ستکنی خوارزم موسوم

کردند و او را پسران بودند پسر بزرگتر قطب الدین محمد او در مرو بمکتب او در پسوم

171

170. Decorated page from a 16th century paper manuscript in Persian, in the Monastery's Library.

171. Miniature illustration from a 13th century parchment manuscript of the Monastery's Library.

172. Illuminated canon-tables of Sunday Readings with the corresponding extracts from the Gospels, from a parchment manuscript of the Monastery's Library. 13th - 14th century.

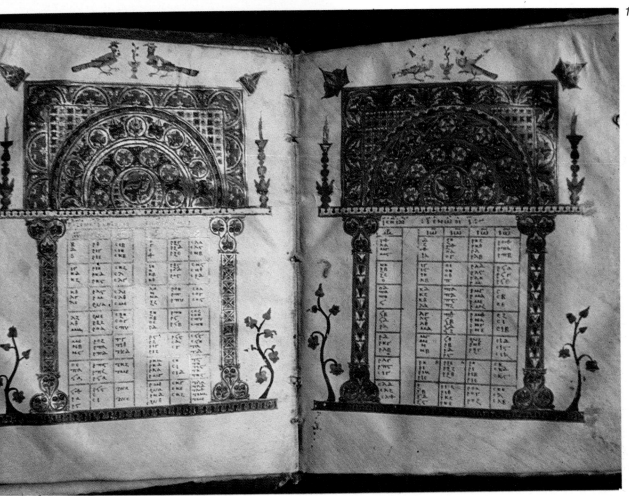

172

173

174

175

176

173.   174.   175.   176.   Miniatures from the illuminated parchment manuscript No. 3 of the Monastery's Library, showing scenes from the sufferings of Job.

177. *A peak of the Mount of St. Episteme, to the north of the Monastery.*

178. *The Justinianic Gate of Confession and part of the long flight of 3,700 steps leading from the Monastery to the summit of the Mount of Moses.*

179

179. The Chapel of St. Catherine on the mountain peak bearing the Saint's name.

180. The Chapel of St. Catherine and the rest-room for pilgrims on the highest summit of the Sinai Peninsula (2,637 m.), which bears the Saint's name. A vision revealed the exact location where her body was found.

181. Imposing view of the Peak of the Decalogue or Mount of Moses (Gabal Mousa, height 2,285 m.) from the even higher summit of the Mount of St. Catherine (Gabal Katerina, height 2,637 m.).

182. The Chapel of the Holy Trinity on the Peak of the Decalogue, built about 50 years ago from ancient material of Justinian's period.

181

182

183. *The sanctuary of the Chapel of St. Catherine, built on the mountain peak bearing the Saint's name.* *Saint's body was miraculously found here and transported to the Monastery of Sinai, thereafter known a* *as St. Catherine's Monastery.*

184. *The Peak of the Decalogue or Mount of Moses. View from the* cathisma *of St. Episteme.*

183

185. *The hermitage of St. Episteme. Ascent to an isolated cave.*

186. *The peak of the Mount of Moses seen from the Mount of St. Episteme.*

187. *The hermitage of St. Episteme and St. Galaktion, recently restored by a hermit monk of Sinai.*

186

187

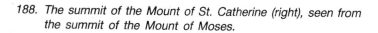

188. *The summit of the Mount of St. Catherine (right), seen from the summit of the Mount of Moses.*

189. *General view of the Monastery from the narrow gorge leading through a flight of 3,700 granite steps to the summit of the Mount of Moses.*

188

190. One of the several holy localities on Mount Horeb, where many hermits lived under the sanctity of the Peak of the Decalogue.

190

191. *Life in an arid, dead landscape, symbolic of the flowering of spiritual life attainable through the death of egoism.*

191

192

193

192. *Monk standing in front of a ruined chapel in the Oasis of Faran (ancient Pharan).*

193. *Plantation of date-palms in the Oasis of Faran, about 60 kms. from St. Catherine's Monastery.*

194. *Plantation of date-palms near El-Tor, the ancient Raitho, at sunset.*

194

195. *The entrance to the garden of the convent at Faran, with St. Catherine's monogram over the door.*

196. *The Chapel of the Prophet Moses in the women's convent in the Valley of Faran.*

197. *Exterior view of the ruined basilica dating from the 5th - 6th century, in the Oasis of Faran.*

198. *Interior view after partial archaeological excavation of the ruined basilica at Faran.*

199. *View of the garden of the women's convent at Faran, from the exonarthex of the Chapel dedicated to the Prophet Moses.*

195 196

197 198

200

201 202

200. *Façade of the Church of St. George in the Monastery's Dependency (Metochi) of the same name on the site of ancient Raitho (the modern El-Tor), where there are still a few Christian Orthodox families under the jurisdiction of the Sinai Archbishopric.*

201. *Interior of a rock-cut chapel on the Red Sea coast, in the vicinity of El-Tor, in the area presently known as Abu-Suera, where hermit monks lived in older times.*

202. *Another chapel, apparently dedicated to St. Demetrios, in the area of Abu-Suera.*

203. St. John Prodromos as angel .

204. *Church of St. George at Raitho. The iconostasis of later date, made and painted by Russian artists.*

205. *The panels of the iconostasis door in the Church of St. George at Raitho.*

204

206. *The Chapel of St. John the Prodrome in one of the valleys of Mount Horeb.*

207. *The Chapel of the True Cross at the locality known as Buaba (i.e. Door). Here, according to tradition, the Israelites fought a battle against the Amalekites, during which Moses was continuously holding his hands raised in prayer, supported by Aaron and Hur, till the final victory of the Israelites over the Amalekites.*

208. The Chapel of the Prophet Aaron, on a small hill by the Valley of the Monastery (Wadi-el-Deir). According to tradition, the Golden Calf was set up and worshipped on this hill.

209. Interior of the Chapel of the Prophet Elijah on Mount Horeb, where the Prophet took refuge fleeing from the wrath of Queen Jezebel, and where he heard the Lord coming unto him as «a still small voice» (I Kings 19, 12).

208

209

210. *The ancient twin chapel dedicated to the Prophets Elijah and Elisha, below the Peak of the Decalogue. It was here at the foot of Mount Horeb that the Prophet Elijah, fleeing from the wrath of Queen Jezebel, took refuge in a cave and heard God as a «still small voice».*

211. *Chapel of St. Panteleimon and garden on Mount Horeb, where many hermits lived.*

212. *Chapel of later date dedicated to St. John Climacus, a 7th century hermit who became abbot of the Monastery of Sinai and wrote the famous ascetic work* Ouranodromos Climax (Ladder to Heaven), *after which he was named.*

213. *Cathisma at the locality known as Bustan, 4 kms. distant from the Monastery of St. Catherine, with a plantation and a chapel honouring the Birth of the Virgin.*

210

211

212

213

214

215

216

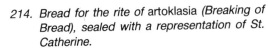

214. Bread for the rite of artoklasia (Breaking of Bread), sealed with a representation of St. Catherine.

215. Bread used for the rite of artoklasia. The representation of the Virgin as the Burning Bush flanked by Moses and St. Catherine has been impressed on the dough by means of a special seal.

216. The small breads ready to be baked in the oven.

217. Making candles for use in the Monastery.

217

220

218. Monks partaking of a meal in the Refectory on a feast day.

219. Scene from the life of the Bedouins in the Monastery. An old monk shares the warmth of their fire, indispensable to them in wintertime.

220. A monk watering the Monastery's orchard and garden. The sparse water must be put into good use and this requires both cost and toil.

218

219

221. *Pilgrim inscriptions in Wadi-el-Hodra.*

222. *Nabataean inscriptions of the 4th - 6th century, in the so-called Valley of Inscriptions (Wadi Mukhattab) near Faran.*

222

223. *Inscriptions in Wadi-el-Hodra (see Pl. 221).*

224. *Pilgrims' inscriptions on granite rocks in Wadi-el-Hodra.*

225. The bell at the entrance to the Monastery. This bell was rung if an emergency occurred during the time when the iron door of the Monastery was customarily closed.

225

226. Springtime on Mount Horeb, symbolic of the eternal spring by the grace of the Holy Ghost – the primary concern and aim of the monastic community.

22

227. Part of the Charnel House of the Monastery, with the piled skulls of deceased monks – «I look for the resurrection of the dead».

228. «Hosios Stephanos» of Sinai. His cadaver dressed in robes sits in a special open casket in the Charnel House of the Monastery. According to the prevailing Sinaitic tradition, he is the one mentioned by St. John Climacus in the «Ladder to Heaven».

229. Sunrise over the granite mass of Mount Horeb. For the hermits of the region it symbolized the hope and beginning of spiritual dawn by the light of Christ's Sun of Justice shining upon their hearts.

230. Sunrise view from the Monastery.

231. Night view of the hostel
and garden of the
Monastery, with the plain
of Raha visible in
the background.

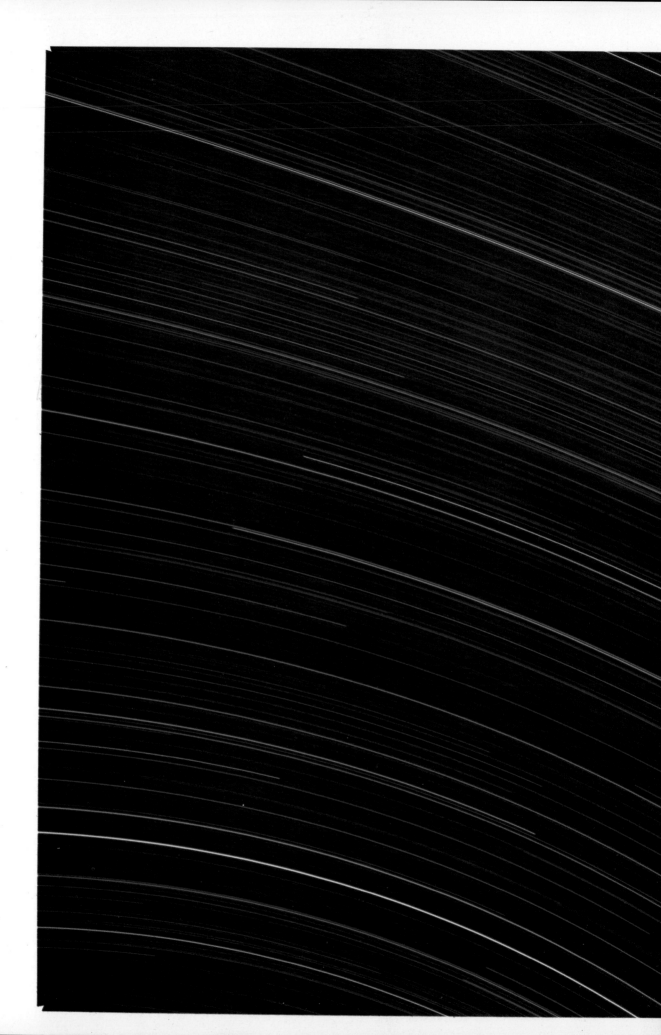

232. Photograph taken from the Monastery showing eight-hour star tracks — «The heavens declare the glory of God; and the firmament sheweth his handywork» (Ps. 19, 1).

233. *Landscape of sand and granite, a work of the strong winds blowing on the Sinai Peninsula.*

234. *Old wooden cross marking a holy locality on Mount Horeb, where hermit monks lived near the monastic habitation of St. Gregory of Sinai.*

23

MAIN BIBLIOGRAPHY

1. Amantos K., Σιναϊτικά μνημεῖα ἀνέκδοτα, Athens, 1928.

2. Amantos K., Σύντομος ἱστορία τῆς Ἱερᾶς Μονῆς τοῦ Σινᾶ, Thessaloniki, 1953, (including main bibliography up to 1953).

3. Bénechévitch W.,Monumenta sinaitica archaeologica et palaeographica. Fasciculus I praefationem editoris, bibliographiam sinaiticam, explicationem tabularum continens, Petrograd, 1925 (including complete bibliography up to 1925).

4. Champdor Albert, Le Mont Sinai et le Monastère Sainte - Catherine, Albert Guillot, Paris 1963.

5. Gregoriades P., Ἡ Ἱερά Μονή τοῦ Σινᾶ κατά τήν τοπογραφικήν, ἱστορικήν καί διοικητικήν αὐτῆς ἔποψιν, Ἐκ τοῦ τυπογραφείου τοῦ Π. Τάφου, Jerusalem, 1875 (Ἐπανεκδίδεται δαπάνη μέν τῆς Ἱερᾶς Μονῆς Σινᾶ, ἐπιμελείᾳ δέ τοῦ Παναγ. Φ. Χριστοπούλου, Athens, 1978).

6. Forsyth H.G. –Weitzmann K., The Monastery of Saint Catherine at Mount Sinai, The University of Michigan Press, 1965.

7. Manousakas M.I., Ἡ ἐπιτομή τῆς Ἱεροκοσμικῆς ἱστορίας τοῦ Νεκταρίου Ἱεροσολύμων καί αἱ πηγαί αὐτῆς, «Κρητικά Χρονικά», Vol. I (1947).

8. Nektarios, Ἐπιτομή τῆς Ἱεροκοσμικῆς ἱστορίας, συγγραφεῖσα παρά τοῦ μακαριωτάτου πρώην Ἱεροσολύμων Πατριάρχου Νεκταρίου τοῦ Κρητός, νεωστί μετατυπωθεῖσα καί μετά πάσης ἐπιμελείας διορθωθεῖσα. Ἐνετίησιν 1805. (First edition 1677, fifth edition 1850).

9. Ouspensky P., First Journey to Sinai in the year 1845. Petrograd 1856 (in Russian).

10. Pantelakis E., Ἡ ἱερά μονή τοῦ Σινᾶ. 1939.

11. Papadopoulos - Kerameus A., Συμβολαί εἰς τήν ἱστορίαν τῆς Ἀρχιεπισκοπῆς τοῦ ὄρους Σινᾶ, Petrograd 1908.

12. Papaioannou E., Ἱερά καί βασιλική Μονή τοῦ Θεοβαδίστου ὄρους Σινᾶ, Ἔκδοσις Ἱερᾶς Μονῆς τοῦ Θεοβαδίστου ὄρους Σινᾶ, 1976.

13. Papamichalopoulos M., Το Μοναστήρι τοῦ Σινᾶ, Athens 1932.

14. Περιγραφή Ἱερά τοῦ Ἁγίου καί Θεοβαδίστου ὄρους Σινᾶ, τυπωθεῖσα νῦν πέμπτον διά δαπάνης τῆς Ἱερᾶς καί βασιλικῆς Μονῆς τοῦ Ἁγίου καί Θεοβαδίστου ὄρους Σινᾶ, Ἐν Βενετίᾳ, παρά Νικολάῳ Γκυκεῖ τῷ ἐξ Ἰωαννίνων, 1817.

15. Porphyrios II, Archbishop of Sinai, Σιναϊτικός Συνέκδημος, Athens 1925.

16. Rabino H., Le monastère de Sainte Catherine du mont Sinai, Cairo 1938.

17. Skrobucha H. – Allan W.G., Sinai, London, New York, Toronto, 1966.

18. Sotiriou G. and M., Εἰκόνες τῆς Μονῆς Σινᾶ, Vol. I (Plates) Athens 1956, Vol. II (Text) 1958.

19. Weitzmann K., The Monastery of St. Catherine at Mount Sinai. The Icons from the 6th - 10th cent., Princeton Univ. Press, Vol. I, N. Jersey 1976.